SOUTHERN TONGUES
LEAVE US SHINING

SOUTHERN TONGUES
LEAVE US SHINING

MARK WAGENAAR

Red Hen Press | Pasadena, CA

Book design by Mark E. Cull

Library of Congress Cataloging-in-Publication Data
Names: Wagenaar, Mark, author.
Title: Southern tongues leave us shining : poems / Mark Wagenaar.
Description: Pasadena, California: Red Hen Press, 2018.
Identifiers: LCCN 2017051791 | ISBN 9781597090360 (tradepaper)
Classification: LCC PS3623.A3523 A6 2018 | DDC 811/.6—dc23
LC record available at https://lccn.loc.gov/2017051791

The National Endowment for the Arts, the Los Angeles County Arts Commission, the Ah-
manson Foundation, the Dwight Stuart Youth Fund, the Max Factor Family Foundation,
the Pasadena Tournament of Roses Foundation, the Pasadena Arts & Culture Commis-
sion and the City of Pasadena Cultural Affairs Division, the City of Los Angeles Depart-
ment of Cultural Affairs, the Audrey & Sydney Irmas Charitable Foundation, the Kinder
Morgan Foundation, the Allergan Foundation, the Riordan Foundation, and the Amazon
Literary Partnership partially support Red Hen Press.

First Edition
Published by Red Hen Press
www.redhen.org

Acknowledgments

My thanks to the editors of these magazines, where these poems first appeared:

Academy of American Poets Poem-A-Day: "They Ate the Bulbs of Tulips"; *Alaska Quarterly*: "Refugee"; *Beloit Poetry Journal*: "Reply to Du Mu from the South"; *Birmingham Poetry Review:* "Appalachian Vowels"; *Boulevard*: "Blue (Southern Exiles)," "Fort Worth Impromptu"; *Colorado Review*: "A Charm for Protection / From the Protectors"; *Field*: "Nocturne with Fitted Absences, Appalachian Farewell"; *Image*: "Texas Blues," "The Trick"; *Mudfish*: "Letteromancy (the New Causality)"; *Narrative Magazine*: "Mississippi Tongues," "Southern Gothic I and II"; *Nimrod*: "Nocturne &/or Aubade with Horses," "Migrations (White Lilacs)," "Stray Paragraphs from the Year of the Rooster"; *Ninth Letter*: "The Oddsmaker (The Little Book of Fate)," "Prayer for This Day," "A Charm for Ghosts (Mississippi Tongues Coda)"; *Raleigh Review*: "Let it Shine on Me," "Silence"; *Ruminate*: "Letter to My Daughter Perhaps Someday," "Southern Tongues Coda (Precision Dying)"; *Sequestrum*: "Southern Divinations II," "Late Sestet"; *Shenandoah*: "Auramancy"; *Soundings East*: "Texas Blues II"; *Southern Indiana Review*: "Nocturne with Horses (Another Exile)," "Ante Up"; *Southern Review*: "Lost Hour Blues," "Southern Reliquaries," "Aubade with Horses (Fort Worth Impromptu II)"; *Southern Humanities Review*: "Southern Update: Triptych," "Drought Blues," "Southern Tongues Leave Us Shining"; *Tar River Poetry*: "Salvage"; *Washington Square*: "Interview with the Last Blacksmith in Mississippi"; *Valparaiso Poetry Review*: "Winter Song".

"Ante Up" was the winner of the 2017 Southern Indiana Review's Mary C. Mohr Poetry Prize, chosen by Maggie Smith.

"Nocturne &/or Aubade with Horses," "Migrations (White Lilacs)," and "Stray Paragraphs from the Year of the Rooster" were part of a batch of poems that won the 2017 Pablo Neruda Prize chosen by Jericho Brown.

"Texas Blues II" was part of a submission that won the 2016 Claire Keyes Poetry Prize, chosen by Ross Gay.

"Southern Update: Triptych," "Drought Blues" and "Southern Tongues Leave Us Shining" were the 2015 winner of the Auburn University Jake Adam York Poetry for Witness Prize, chosen by Richard Tillinghast.

"String Theory" was the 2015 CBC National Poetry Prize winner.

"Nocturne with Horses (Another Exile)" was the winner of the 2014 Southern Indiana Review's Mary C. Mohr Poetry Prize, chosen by Marie Howe.

"Letteromancy (the New Causality)" was the runner-up in the 2015 Mudfish Poetry Prize, chosen by Edward Hirsch.

"Mississippi Tongues" was part of a suite that took second runner-up in the 2014 Narrative Magazine Poetry Awards, and were published therein.

Though I'll always forget someone who deserves it, I wanted to take a shot at saying thanks: To my beloved, Chelsea Marie, where do I begin; to my daughter, Eloise Virginia, aka Weezy—if you read this, years hence, I hope it will be obvious how your life irrevocably changed ours, in uncountable ways—we're so grateful for your life; to my folks, Fred and Kathy; my brothers Jesse, Benny, Joshie, and their families; to Nana, my sisters Ris and Alaina, and to my brother Kyler; to Aldemar and family; Gertje Wagenaar—our dearly loved and greatly-missed Beppe, and Pake; Canada family; Gary Link, grandfather, whom we miss, and Millie; NJ fam; Bruce Bond, from whom I learned so much at UNT; Corey Marks, another cherished poet, UNT professor, and friend; B.H. Fairchild—"Pete"—fellow pilgrim, who helped us mourn Giddy from two thousand miles away; kindred spirit Mark Irwin; Matthew Callender, fellow writer and artist; the Blockers; Beth Ann Fennelly (and her sweet family), for reading this book, and for choosing me—and my poems—for the Ole Miss Summer Poet-in-Residence, where this book began; to Ole Miss—my thanks. What a place; Wisconsin folks: Amaud Johnson, Ron Wallace, Amy Quan Barry, Jesse Lee Kercheval, Sean Bishop; the Red Hen folks—Kate Gale, Hannah Moye, Keaton Maddox, and the rest of the crew, I'm just amazed by your kindness, expertise, and professionalism—and your patience; my thanks to "Traces of Texas," a Facebook page run by an anonymous big-hearted well-travelled Texan, who regularly posts historical stories of Texas; those sweet Clarks, GD and E; Richard Sévère; and the Valpo folks, my thanks.

Contents

Introduction   1

I. Dark Was the Night / Cold Was the Ground

Refugee   5

Southern Gothic I   7

Nocturne with Horses (Another Exile)   8

Southern Gothic II   12

Blue (Southern Exiles)   13

Migrations (White Lilacs)   15

The Oddsmaker (The Little Book of Fate)   17

Reply to Du Mu from the South   18

A Charm for Protection / from the Protectors   20

Diptych: Self-Portrait with Hundreds of Horse Skulls (Solve for X)   23

Fort Worth Impromptu   25

II. Trouble Will Soon Be Over

Mississippi Tongues: a Poem in Nine Parts   29

    I. Southern Divinations   31

    II. *What's the Last Thing that Goes Through a Bug's Head* 33

    III. Southern Locution (Erasures)   35

    IV. Mama Jan's Advice for This Life   36

    V. Issaquena County Blues (Theology)   38

    VI. Interview with the Last Blacksmith in Mississippi   39

    VII. Natchez Trace Ecstatic   41

    VIII. String Theory   43

    IX. A Charm for Ghosts (Mississippi Tongues Coda)   46

Lost Hour Blues   48

Salvage   50

Drought Blues   51

Ante Up   53

Winter Song   55

Texas Blues   57

Southern Tongues Leave Us Shining   60

III. Bye & Bye I'm Going to See the King

Appalachian Vowels   65

Auramancy   67

Reliquaries   70

Silence   73

Nocturne with Fitted Absences   75

Appalachian Farewell   77

The Trick   78

IV. Sweeter as the Years Go By

Southern Update: Triptych   83

Letter to My Daughter Perhaps Someday   88

Nocturne &/or Aubade with Horses   90

V.   Let Your Light Shine on Me

Southern Divinations II   95

How Does a Man Become a Hashtag   97

They Ate the Bulbs of Tulips   100

Prayer for This Day   101

Late Sestet   104

Let It Shine on Me   105

Southern Tongues Coda (Precision Dying)   107

Texas Blues II   109

Stray Paragraphs from the Year of the Rooster   111

Letteromancy (The New Causality)   115

Aubade with Horses (Fort Worth Impromptu II)   117

SOUTHERN TONGUES
LEAVE US SHINING

Introduction

Begin with a river. Such is the image that feeds the image of the southern tongue, as Mark Wagenaar conceives it. Begin with a departure and the name of the river it leaves behind. What the poets forge of this moment is a myth: the passing of the dead between the banks of what remains. What we find is a liminal space between irrevocable loss and stubborn reassertion. Of what, we ask? We ask again. Southern tongues (as they leave us) shine, as we shine in turn to mourn their leaving. Easy to say. But the brilliance of Wagenaar's book lies less in the turn from grief to affirmation, less in the reassurance of an answer, than in the deep, abiding complexity of the mind that questions. Language appears as constituted of questions, however realized the diaspora, local the vantage, magnanimous the land.

Any wonder then the book opens with a refugee, a spirit caught in a body, between worlds, haunted by the fading of a native tongue that never entirely fades. The nine-pound hammer of the human heart is decidedly American, however foreign this America, however bitter, to the one who claims it in story and song. We could say, with some accuracy, that exile is the natural state of the poet. The imagination seeks to realize greater and greater participation in the past that made it, the one it lost, the one it is on the cusp of losing. That said, the ghosts that illuminate *Southern Tongues* long to be singular. They want to be set apart, named as bodies are, and yet (and so) bound by lineage and tongue to some larger order. The restless enormity of Wagenaar's reach in these poems, the resourcefulness that makes its unities of such scatterings of culture, such agonies of servitude, dream-like awakenings of loss, embodies the longing to be ever more particular and yet inclusive, generous and yet unsentimental about the limits of a poet's means.

Thus the light of his vision is ever out there, in the world, and in the stubborn absence the world leaves behind. But likewise, it is a deep inwardness that teaches us to care. "We come to know the world as a veil learns a face," he writes, and thus, with characteristic speed and energy of resonance, he images the immanent unknown, its proximity to mourning, if not marriage, its face that gazes through us, as we, irrevocably, have looked. The deeply imaginative realism of the book refuses to expurgate its dreams. The voice and details of the speaker's life remind us history is a local experience. Its context is the eye it passes through. Like a thread through a needle. To be clear, the story cannot be too clear. To be alive, it must remain undone. It must honor a certain measure of the ineffable in the all too sure. "Give it time," Wagenaar says of the past. "Soon the faces / will begin to surface // like coins, like a well // giving up its wishes." To "give up" as in "relinquish" or "make manifest." To leave and, in departure, come, by deep analogy, to mind.

—Bruce Bond

I
DARK WAS THE NIGHT
COLD WAS THE GROUND

Refugee

the horse's spirit dwells in its body

the way an eclipse burns in a pinholed matchbox

like the syllables inside a prayer

wind-shucked snow devils race across the snow

then a current ripples across the skin-shimmer

mane to hoof

& the horse organs—   lung-bellows
& nine-pound heart

flatten as the body arrows across the field

toward the gate at the end

open to the half-frozen river

only the head heart & hooves will be buried

if it was escape that brought you here
where will you go

if you are the lone glyph that the language
of vanishing has left behind

what will you sing

Southern Gothic I

At some point the empty rooms become you.

The days fall into each other.

The crickets pile up beside the gas pumps

like the husks of shattered violins.

They're laid down with our sorry words, our five & dime apologies.

The faces around you shuttle by so fast they flicker

like heat lightning above the treeline.

At some point it all comes back to you.

The Union gunboat fires on retreating black soldiers,

instead of the charging Confederates.

At some point you give up on the missing.

At some point you're at the mercy of what's hidden in the heart of man.

How do you wrap your heart around that?

At some point the river gives up its bones.

Nocturne with Horses (Another Exile)

for Tommy

If death is a dialogue between spirit & dust,
it is the horses who will speak for the spirit
on our behalf—

        sometimes more spirit than flesh,

the way they'll spook at a movement or a scent
that is unseen, that is either beyond us

or not there at all, a wisdom
beyond the sense of flesh, what flesh might be capable of—

the way they'll stand at attention
in evening's afterrain mists rising from the hot earth

& quiver as if an electric current rippled through their flank,

as if small arrows of light were constantly loosed into the starry horse sky
their wet skin holds,
until you approach, until they're sure you pose no threat.

The breath of these two just beyond the three-tiered pine fence
is quiet as the word *exile*

        in a recitation of the Torah,
which tells us that even God is pleased
with horses, with their wind tunnel-licked form,

            their riverine shine,

but they are quiet when you ask them of their maker,

                                       who numbers their days

& ours, or about the hereafter,
because they might just know something
since fourteen of their kin were buried on a Norse longboat
with a queen, & five hundred terra cotta models

in Emperor Qin's necropolis (beneath a ceiling painted
with heavenly bodies, Sima Qian tells us

from twenty centuries away, buried with jade & gold,
towers, even officials, amidst one hundred rivers of mercury).

But these horses say nothing about this day,
or your life, or the one brother in three

who will be locked away this year in this state—
if the stats hold,
               & they will—
at Leakesville, & Central Miss, & Parchman Farm,
home to Unit 29, Mississippi's Death Row.

And because you believe in mercy,
that if it is to exist somewhere

it must be what we can make of this moment,
that eventually you must trust your life to something

                                        larger than your life,
you pluck the white eyeballs

of engorged ticks from their flanks—
you lean your entire body into your thumbnail & fingernail
so they press a half-inch into this horse's skin
                                        to tear away the tick head
fanged in the horse flesh.

And because leaving them in the field is to give the horses back to them,
you gather them in your hands
like a strange harvest
                    of white strawberry-sized cataracts,
carry them to a nearby rock still warm from the departed sun,

& though you understand that this is only another form
of survival,
& though you understand their exile from the horse body

(because you have stood, stunned,
against a storefront window while you were frisked,
& saw in your own dark skin a lineage

that stretches back to another continent, back
to a body that body could not call his own,
back to a salt furnace, coal mine, shotgun shack with dirt floors
                                        & forward

to a robbery beef, an assault rap,
forward to another exile:
your father's sixty months at the Farm—
saw your own long term someday),

you heft his nine pound hammer
& strike the ticks where they lie on the rock

so the white bags burst in great sparks of horse blood,

until the rock's as wet as the moment
of Agamemnon's last cry.

Southern Gothic II

At some point the river gives up its bones.

How do you wrap your heart around that?

At some point you're at the mercy of what's hidden in the heart of man.

At some point you give up on the missing.

Instead of the charging Confederates,

the Union gunboat fires on retreating black soldiers.

At some point it all comes back to you:

like heat lightning above the treeline

the faces around you shuttle by so fast they flicker;

they're laid down with our sorry words, our five & dime apologies.

Like the husks of shattered violins

the crickets pile up beside the gas pumps.

The days fall into each other.

At some point the empty rooms become you.

Blue (Southern Exiles)

Quiet as the applause of ghosts
three horses sidle up to us at the white fenceline,

one for each Alamo pyre.

Body of embers,
the way they glow, it's said
Seguin returned a year later,

as the story goes,
unearthed bits of bone & handfuls
of ashes into a coffin, & buried it all
beneath a peach tree grove
while the bells rang out in San Fernando.

And after they'd been laid rest,
the grave was forgotten.
Just the way of the world,
we forget & don't notice

the absence forgetting makes.
Little spaces. Like those in the dog's paws
when you pull the cactus needles clear,

or the burnspots in the welder's hands
where the sparks burned through the gloves.

Names drift from the earth—
like this blue smoke that follows the fireworks.
Round blue frames waiting for their faces.

An orderly cortège of blue shades
above these quiet horses,
who stay despite the explosions.

God, a courage like theirs
when all's gone to shit,

a Thy-will-be-done faith
despite all fuckery, a faith
in the face of the world's end.

The nuns sang in Galveston
to calm the children
during the hurricane—
sang as the water rose higher.
Sang until the children joined in.

Migrations (White Lilacs)

What sense of lack says open this ground,
this is where the white lilacs go,

open the window, it's snowing, therefore
the shadows from Sonny Stitt's horn

bop their way down the street, a migration
like the journey of the old runes,
                                    thorn, eth & ash et al.,
that traveled across the years, through dreams
& sacked cities
                    to become Old English letters,
or that of the words inside this phone,
where a bit of want bends

the letters, so *experience* autocorrects to *corrientes* (ocean
or electric currents, common, or running),
going somehow becomes *gnosis*—
                                    isn't the gnosis of going
all about loss? And it is, for all of us.
For my kin, almost all gone from Friesland, where we hail.
And it is, if it's Frisian, the language
of our fathers & mothers
few in our family speak now.

And it is—if it's here a hundred years ago in Denton,
where the black families of Quakertown were forced across the tracks:

houses bumped at a rattler's pace on the rollers:
one woman, Mary Ellen, refused to leave her house,
& sat in her parlor rocking chair the whole journey,
while her Henry jogged alongside the house:

they started again with their lack,
with cuttings from their white lilac bushes.

Lilacs to lilacs, drift of lost vowels, is it grief or need that blooms
in the wound opened by these distances?
Spaces made of the want they're opened by,

by the years that fall through us soundlessly,
endlessly, like the snow outside,
                                        white petals upon the air.

The Oddsmaker (The Little Book of Fate)

Turns out you can bet on anything—whether Monica Lewinsky or Big Bird will
be mentioned in a debate, if your son will grow up to play for Manchester United. I
wonder how one handicaps the chicken bingo game, or accounts for Paul the Octo-
pus' perfect record in choosing World Cup winners. What were the odds that the
diary of the first Israeli astronaut would survive the Columbia explosion & a
hundred mile freefall, so that the Kaddush blessing would be read by crickets in
Palestine, Texas? Or the odds that a man who visits a courthouse in Gonzalez a
hundred miles from the impact, & runs his hand over the names scratched in the
wood of death row, would find his own name engraved there, the last man hung in
the town? What were the odds Albert Howard was guilty? Don't ask, the man is
told when he asks. He was black, & this was a long time ago. The courthouse clock
the man looks upon has never worked since. He draws a line between the name in
the wood & his own. Now Albert is looking at the courthouse with different eyes.
It's strange, he says, but I almost remember now. This was my last day. The horse
pulling the wagon that would take me away. The sunlight through the red dust
clouding up from the street. The chime of the clock striking the hour a last time.

Reply to Du Mu from the South

Du Mu looks up from a letter he's writing to us

                                  twelve centuries ago,
a letter edged with a description of the four hundred eighty temples
of the Southern dynasties—
what they did with their idleness,

with a need they couldn't explain.

Old friend, the same wind
that lifted the corners of the rice paper

                           around your hand
rifles wild white yarrow & black-eyed Susans
in the field beyond the burned church.

Here, as many empty porches & boarded windows as Southern temples.
Tractors rust to grass, county roads dissolve to gravel,

                                 the walkers on the bridge
vanish. Where do they go,
the ones who move on without a word,
who leave toys in the back yard, utility bills on the front door?

Here, a little sunshine & a winedark spill of deer's blood

                               across the county line,
orange sun-spotted pagodas
of wild tiger lilies in the ditches

off the rain-tamped white dust of Elk Chapel Road,

                                              a straight shot to the polestar.

So much I can't explain,

                        so much forgotten or unfinished,

if you can tell the two apart.

Old friend, I'll be forgotten.

A Charm for Protection
from the Protectors

"Assume the position—
stop look & listen"
—*"The What," Notorious B.I.G. & Method Man*

Because it's not enough for your son
to have a platelet count of one hundred,

because once his bilirubin levels fall
he will have to leave the tent

of light he lies beneath, little
phosphorescent idol, neon glowworm

with capillaries & aortas & aqueducts
a thousand times more complicated

than the uncounted tracheal tubes
within the butterfly's chrysalis,

because he will be made, one day,
to lie facedown in the street, nose & lips

to asphalt, & you can only dream the ark
of feathers, the Kevlar-stitched

cradle (even holding the half-god
by his heels & dipping him in the Styx

did not work: we are vulnerable
at the place we are held),

because beyond teaching him to raise
his hands slow, slow, to say *sir*

when he hears *boy*, there is nothing
else you can do, say his name

to the spillway pulsing with last night's
rain, repeat his blood type

to the wind, alive now in its wounds
of petunias & honeysuckle.

Leave the last lock of his first haircut
in the empty mouth of the lone

Confederate statue in the town square.
Rub out the oracle figures in the blood

that rivulets the asphalt
from the deer hanging by its heels

in a driveway. Press yourself against
a net of thistles & stones, against

your shadow, which holds the shadow
of a boy falling, the shadows

of flowers piled in the street
are falling like rain through

the bare rafters in the house
that is his future, the rafters your hands

are holding up, your hands
are counting his ribs, each rib.

Diptych: Self-Portrait with Hundreds of Horse Skulls (Solve for X)

after Oliver de la Paz

Place is called Horsehead Crossing,
first used by Comanches, the man in the seat
next to me said as we crossed the Pecos River,

a surveyor found hundreds of horse skulls here—
drank too deep from the river after going too hard
too long. I never know what to say back—

you know this feeling? Talking about nothing
until nothing's enough, a way to pass the miles & hours,
one version
                of Derrida's infinite deferral
of whatever it is again, maybe trivia
shows us the limit of what we know,
                           marginalia
of our inattention, our haste, ghost of the god
of knowledge, who walks the desert barefoot,
                             an X to solve for
if it's Charades or Pictionary,
                  I never know
what disclosure will suffice, credit score
or what I owe the IRS, letter I began the day
                      my daughter was born,
dog's name & breed, that dog that won't spook

'till a body acts spooked around him—

                              creep forward, hesitant, one hand up—
but enough about me on payday

                        or at the Lord's Table

(X is a freedman who fought for the Confederates

X is the favorite flower of Pissarro's wife

X wonders how to hallow the space in a tree

                              after a body's been taken down

X once said they all have the same name & the name is lost

X said to the devil you want to see how the sausage is made? Consider my servant Job

X is listening for hoofbeats as the shades of twilight walk westward

X is the date of Juneteenth

X has opened all the secret windows & every peony in town has bloomed at once).

Fort Worth Impromptu

If heaven's a boosted Caddy
language is the pair of tin cans
with which we've been listening
                              for the LoJack signal,
one to our ear, one held up to the air: nothing

for a while now, aside from a little static.
Nothing, at least, outside this slaughterhouse,
                                        where I walk a picket line
some seventy years after everyone's moved on—
doors chained shut, bone saw long quiet,
                              rust-seized & skull-still.
I drop by once in a while to listen for my lineage—
my grandmother's father was a butcher in Holland,

& when the Nazis forbade the slaughter of animals—
people were eating tulip bulbs—
did it anyways. Blade to throat, wind-quick.
Once, during a search, my grandmother hid a sheep's heart in her bed.

Boys surf the hoods of driverless cars
down the side streets of redlined neighborhoods west of here,
where last week a horse tore headstall from halter
& bolted for it, in a city

where thousands of horses once walked,
thousands a day—quicksilver glistening, mane & eye—
then they were gone.
A little light in my grandmother's eyes, & now it's gone.

I was a thousand miles away,
                              a day late & a buck short.
A week since I, with five of my cousins, carried her home—
who asked me three months ago, where, Mark,

                              is God in the long night.
What do you say to an unending wakefulness?

Hold what you got, Joe Tex said, today
                              forty-four years dead.
Hold what you got, even if you don't know
where your heart is hid, if you're as haunted
as heaven might be

by those forever absent,

those who didn't make it through the gates,
as this evening sky is haunted
                              by the body we trace in the stars,
God or the ghost of God
ghost-riding nothing's whip.

II
TROUBLE WILL SOON BE OVER

MISSISSIPPI TONGUES:
A POEM IN NINE PARTS

I am going, Deacon Jones
I went down to the church house
I got down on my bended knee
I prayed, I prayed all night, I prayed
Deacon Jones, pray for me

—John Lee Hooker, "Burnin' Hell"

I feel my body, my bones and flesh beginning to part and open upon the alone,
and the process of coming unalone is terrible.

—Dewey Dell, *As I Lay Dying*

I. Southern Divinations

The signs are everywhere. The cat drops headless birds, cardinal,
bluejay, something whitewinged, beside the rocker on the front porch.

A diamondback leaves its skin at field's edge. Heaps of dead wasps
near it, sun-brindled bodies like a funeral pyre in time's slow flame.

A perfect circle of feathers: yes, you'll owe more than you have today.
A perfect circle of raised white welts: yes, there will be enough

for dinner tonight. You find a one-antlered deer skull hung
from the branches of a young oak: yes, she'll come back someday.

Bag worms like prayer lanterns at wood's edge, sizzle
of cicadas in the trees, a hundred ratchets spinning on the car

of the dog-bayed August sun. The signs are everywhere. The dogs
got another one of the chickens. A mimosa drops its flares

into the river, the light of years resurfacing reaches you. The light
of other towns. Other tongues, older tongues. *Issaquena*, Choctaw

for *deer river*. You say it to the crumpled deer body roadside,
tiger lilies blazing on their wicks in the ditch. *Issaquena*.

The first two county seats are now ghost towns on this alluvial plain,
buckshot soil, bottomland. Ghost towns, ghost tongues, we, too,

are alluvial, & bear the traces of others upon us. *This county is no*
dry bones, this county will rise again, our neighbor rumbles, the one who wears

a gator's tooth around his neck for luck. Seven types of fog, seven types
of rattlers. Ache of crepe myrtle blossoms by the road, white ones, fuchsia,

ache of all we cannot bring ourselves to ask: pocketless, starless,
what can a body keep, what can a body bear? You must ask yourself,

the river, the dark, you must ask a hundred times, because so many
have gone into both without an answer. Benthic ourselves,

alluvial, we bear the signs, names, petals, ashes of a church fire
on the air, we bear the light of names no one knows how to say anymore.

II. *What's the Last Thing that Goes Through a Bug's Head*

when it hits the windshield—
                                        the attendant asks
at the last station before the two-lane blacktop
hits the Natchez Trace: foot-smoothed path
from Natchez to Nashville: hundred-foot pines,
Pegasus & Lyra-blossomed magnolia, crepe myrtles
like burning cars roadside: his half-limp almost
the same as my father's,
                                        arthritis in his knee radiating
like starlight in water: a riddle with an answer,
one we ask instead of asking about our own
last words, last questions, even at this lonely
outpost, where rusty ceiling fans chase their tails
all day, & a mini pagoda of disposable cameras,
each with their own
                                        empty window, wait
for a figure to wave back at us: the Bible opened
on the counter to a dog-eared Psalm 88,
*& mahalath leannoth (to be read at the suffering
of afflictions)* circled in red: a lineage that begins
with a half-limp, & goes back generations
of Primitive Baptists,
                                        Hard Shell Baptists,
back to a man owned by another: lineage, the falling
of one day into the next: what we are heir to,
what we are at the mercy of: Old Trace, what flickers
in the blood? : something kin to the twenty centuries

of dark in the Pharr Mounds, burial tumuli a few miles
from this place:
                    something like the sixth taste
on the tongue, or the seventh, if it exists: unanswerable:
how long this season of white hair, how long
will Yahweh stay silent: how much of this galaxy's
light, this river of heaven, is the light of white dwarfs:
dead stars: where else do death & eros collide
in the world: burst sacks
                            of thistle still on the stalk
bulge like eyeballs in the next field, waiting
for the right wind out of the cypress swamps
to carry the seeds: as we wait, halfhearted, off-balance,
for something beyond us to carry us, to get us
through another day, to bear these frailties—

                                    its ass.

III. Southern Locution (Erasures)

Even now the letters & syllables begin to

Ravel themselves around their own disappearances

As the speakers forget them: *Mephis, Missippi*:
                                                  like phantom limbs, like a
Shroud of fingerprints lifted from arrowheads

Underneath the bodies. This is how a place vanishes. The letters

Rise toward names already beyond the horizon.

Even now they dissolve on our tongues, *James Chaney, Andrew Goodman, Michael*

Schwerner . . .

IV. Mama Jan's Advice for This Life

Grief's a drowned palomino, all fifteen hands of her.
We'll spend our days tracing those hands on this gravel road

off a gravel road off county blacktop. All the names return
at day's end, whitetail hour, with the tiger lilies dying in a ditch,

all them boys still missing, their mouths full of moonlight
& Issaquena County clay. Go on, do a Google search:

the first three it suggests are *Issaquena County jail MS,*
Issaquena County jail, & Issaquena County prison.

The boys may as well drive their snorting short boxes
& half tons (half-pints of clear shine beneath the seat)

right through the glittering barbed wire. If there's a hole
in heaven's side, it's been worn in a little at a time,

like the Natchez Trace, worn in with our bodies.
When the children grow up, they'll break

your heart, don't kid yourself. Because everyone else will.
We've seven types of rattlers, & how many kinds of luck?

That's all you got in a county of bottomland forest
in buckshot soil, & water on the way to the Delta. Find somebody.

All you are is a confluence of needs. My Earl,
he once brought me a glass of water when I was coughing

in the middle of the night, wrapped in the T-shirt he was wearing.
Find somebody that tender. Two hundred years too late

for the Choctaw, maybe it's not too late for us. There's plenty
of shades in these woods for the shoes left on the porch.

V. Issaquena County Blues (Theology)

And God gives, Mama, the way bridges do—
gives out when you're halfway across.
There's a hole in heaven where some sin slips through,

& that's where the Mississippi's rolling to.
Some place that forgets, somewhere beyond our loss.
And even God gives, the way guitar strings do:

sounds our lives as the earth's sounded by the dew.
Too many turned out, laid up, hospice or big house.
But there's a hole in heaven where some sin slips through,

so make a break if you see it, the way crows
go for the eyes first. Might be redemption in the dross
because God can give, Mama, the way beauty do—

gives back the pieces it took, less a few:
drowned horses & petals, those beyond breath or shoes.
There's a hole in heaven where some sin slips through—

& one or two of us might slip out of Issaquena too.
We're left with hard luck, hard prayer, & a high cross.
Because even God gives out, the way hearts do—
but there's a hole in heaven where some sin slips through.

VI. Interview with the Last Blacksmith in Mississippi

What did you make?
A perfect coin, that bears no face, that will balance on any eyelid.
A weightless blade to cut the nooses down from the trees.

How did you learn your craft?
The earth is a beautiful sieve: we are what has been caught.
I saw how hunger curved the coyote's ribs.

No, how did you learn your craft?
I bore a thorn in my palm for seven days.
I smoothed ashes upon the river & watched the gray oracle figures disappear.

What did you dream?
A forge beyond the sparks of the stars. The faces on the cooling waters . . .
I traced the Hand that traced us first.

How did you forget?
I watched steel break like glass.
What are the stars but furnaces? What is between them but all we've forgotten?

No, how did you forget?
I unlearned by holding a bracelet of hair.
I weighed the white bones of the disappeared.

Where are you going?
Where the thrown arrowhead points.
I hear the river whistle ahead of its bones.

What will you leave us?
A metal softer than flesh, lighter than song or shadow.
We come to know the world as a veil learns a face.

VII. Natchez Trace Ecstatic

Someone pulls the cork
                            & the evening amberlight drains through the cypress,
mimosa blooms shimmering like the blur of hands
before the *abracadabra*

& the day disappears,
the way the congregation of this abandoned
white clapboard church did.

Here, some hundred miles from the twin-cabined dogtrot where Lewis died
by his own hand
                        or another's,
no one's sure,
these Hard Shell Baptists, the old school's old school,

refused even instruments in their worship:
anything except voice was mere decoration.

And beyond this place bent on a place beyond
(some had one eye on heaven
                                    & one peeled for revenuers)
the Old Trace begins, footworn path, begun by hunters
who followed herds
                        to Tennessee salt licks,
if the story holds,
the same way the hollow in heaven's side,
                                    if it's still there,

has been worn in a little at a time,

                                             its heart unreachable.

In the encroaching woods behind the church,

                                        slash pine, longleaf, red elm & bitter pecan,

black moths unlip from the dark

near a pond hidden in the long grass like a stolen kidney.

Here hard prayer began like a thirst

                             for salt.

Here they laid their old selves in the water,

                                 this Mississippi mudpuddle

become a river Jordan,

become another self as the fog lifts from it,

                                 translucent as the next life.

No voices here any longer,

only skeeters on an air that was once hymn-haunted—

because there's nothing ornamental in this place,

here we resemble what we've lost,

become a palimpsest of what's missing.

Here the cotton shall rise again like white tongues,

                                    white Pentecostal flames, & the body,

the body shall gutter in our mouths,

the wounds sound our depths,

                            & the rattler prove our faith.

VIII. String Theory

You should know how to jump a car,
& how to change a tire, my father once told me.
To that I'd add where to buy the best shine
in town, which is always out of someone's trunk.
In Oxford, look for an '89 Cherokee,
rust-mottled white, & tinted dark as ink,
because a woman named Chaz will sell a jelly jar
with hardly a charcoal speck. She's a disciple
of string theory—not the one that says strings
send their 2D worldsheet through spacetime,
one candidate for The Theory of Everything—
but the shine version: she plays an old violin
in a barn to the sealed jars & a horse, Bill.
They don't have ears, she says, maybe the vibrations
soften the shine some. She's got her own set
of must-knows: how to make an easy grand
hauling cigarettes across state lines, how to grow
your own blue corn for the stuff. How to kick
the other stuff, blue flame, burn spoon, dying horse
or heroin, the appetite goes first, she says.
You should know what it's like to bury
a horse, to spend a morning digging a piano-size
grave, for twenty cents. Three jars in, she tells me
something. We wrapped chains around one
that got stuck in a drinking hole. Her rump in the air,
chunks of horse flesh missing: coyotes
we'd hear at night as we drifted off to sleep.
When the chains tightened as the tractor heaved

the mare's belly gave, & her body was pulled
from a womb-wet colt. You should know
some things stay with you the rest of your life.
I even saw that colt as I held up the ultrasound pic
the first time, she says. The birth of your first-born
will wreck every part of you. And I know this.
I've held that picture in my hands. I've heard
that heart, that stunning wingbeat on the speaker,
that otherworldly whistling, an ambulance passing
by you, if you're stretchered out in the back
at the same time. Like hearing a helicopter
underwater, or talking to a friend on the phone
when he's in freefall. I should know by now I'll never
know all the strings that pull me this way or that.
I mean thirst, & history, mistakes & all, I mean
the way we become our parents, so I know enough
to know I don't know shit, but that heartbeat,
that unborn heartbeat did to me what the late train horn
does to the plains, what the blood moon does
to midnight. This week of her first dreams, body
in Golden Mean proportions already, like Chaz's violin.
Zeising once measured the body & found a 3:2 ratio
in length, which is a Perfect Fifth on a scale—
so who sang us into being, who first struck our hearts
into rivering with a few slides along the strings?
Even this beauty is an eyelash next to the end we share.
All I see, all I hope to, is a length of days past
mine when I look hard at the ultrasound clouds,

at the face upon the waters. The way Chaz looks
at the sun too long sometimes, so the burnspots spark,
then coalesce, until a blueblack colt walks out of the sun.

IX. A Charm for Ghosts (Mississippi Tongues Coda)

Blue smoke on the marrow horizon line,
heaven's half-ton a quart low,
                              burning a little oil as it goes
across the Yocona. Always just beyond us,
dead languages pinned like butterflies in its trunk,
                              its haul of dead tongues,
a shade riding shotgun.
A ways below, mine won't be quiet.
I have my dead & I have let them go, it says.

The grief that I hear is my life's echo,
but what it hears is beyond me.

Death row inmates banging on their bars
in solidarity this Day Of.
A mother hearing her son's heart beat in the chest of another,
                              faint as a moondog's cry.
The sound of the year passing, another year at war,

but they say there'll be an end to the turning of the years.
They say the angel of history is blindfolded,
                              & around here
they say a child's first gun should be an AK,
                              it's that hard to screw up.
Hard for me to imagine.
Except maybe for guns,
a thousand years ago they had a charm for almost everything.

A charm for the journey. One against bees.
One for the white wings falling
                              through evening's corn silk shine,
dove season. Someone above the bag limit,
if I counted the shots right.
One for the sound of the next life,
rattle of cicadas in the trees, fragments of bone
                              in a tin cup.
Æcerbot, the Field Remedy, for unfruitful lands—
but this land has seen such a yield
                              of strange fruit.
A charm for everything, except maybe for ghosts.
And where would you begin.
A litany of earth & sky & eros,
baptisia alba, cumulonimbus, white camellia,
skin-at-your-lover's heel,
                    dark of the larynx.
If you love this world, the Good Book says,
                              love of the Father is not in you,
but I don't know that I can help it,
the body of the world I love begins with the body
                              of the last one missing.
I have my dead & I have let them go.
The grief that I hear is my life's echo.

Lost Hour Blues

It's *departure* inscribed on the air in the October evening,
six & ten foot flights of grasshoppers arcing across vacant lots
gone to seed, the wakes & screws & contrails
                             of falling leaves
& planes circling DFW & Love Field.

Somewhere out there is the step I lost between my twenties & thirties
Somewhere the last word my wife said in sleep is still echoing.
And the hour we lost between Santa Fe & Dallas must be somewhere above

this woman busking a waterless spillway of grasshoppers
                             & skateboard pilgrims
in a town where the calls of distant trains meet at last.
What an embarrassment of riches she has
                      to pick on her guitar—
three year drought blues, or seventeen year,
depending on who you ask.

The lifted truck blues, rollin' coal blues, both barrels,
                         duallies & half tons & short boxes.
The AR blues, extended mag blues.
Skeeter bite blues, the West Nile roulette we play
                    each time we take a walk,
toxic subprime loans blues, & more underwater mortgages
in these neighborhoods than Atlantis, if we ever find it.

And aside from the fracking blues & the little earthquakes
                      that attend us,

48

is there anything in the blues of the ten thousand places
on the disappeared,
or the lone child migrant
                              no one seems to know what to do with,
is there anything from that catalogue
for dove season,
some evernote alive in this afterlife of autumn
                                        to trace the score the white wings
leave
on the air as they plunge.
I keep hoping for something after last call,
                                    in this twilight's
twilight, something more, some grace I won't recognize
'till it has a hold of me,

some turn card, some *other* I can't explain, a mark
the ineffable leaves upon us,
                              faint as the white tails that ghost through
cattle rail & thicket & steel fence,
                                through lost hours
& last words,
more flame than flesh, more flicker
                              than tongue,
like the translucent bodies, the ones past all pain,
the radiant ones the preachers say we're migrating to.

Salvage

The salvage yard's forty acres of brokedown
busted-up wrecks, where we once got fifty bucks
for our grocery getter, an '89 wagon.
My father & I stalk aisles of cars & trucks

for replacement parts—rims, belts, compressor.
Pops a hood—holds a lighter up in the skull,
runs a hand along the radiator.
Nothing lasts, but nothing's irreplaceable—

except for the faulty parts he passed down.
Same lousy knees, leaky valves—blood flow
half-slowed in his Gremlin heart. Same depression,

same blown hippocampus. All this, yet a grin
when he sees the old 'Vette: sixteen again, all show
& fro, gunning down Main St for the horizon.

Drought Blues

Out of the perfect circles of feathers
on lawns & roadsides,

out of the rotting maws of javelinas,
from the bowed heads of wilting wildflowers,

from bathtub rings around lakes,
& the exposed Indian graves once in twenty feet of water

the drought rises to walk amongst us,
                                        white hair
& translucent skin a sheer rippling

above the trees, body of vapor & heat,
limbic shadows knotting
& untying beneath the bean & pecan trees.

Diminish, diminish, it says
with its mouth full of feathers,
                              hot finger in my mouth,
in the mouths of every one of the yet-to-be-transfigured.

What do we mean by shelter, it asks us,
the same question castoff shoes
& empty gallon bottles in ranch fields ask us.

Add that to the others we're in the midst of answering—
how far north do the narcocorridos carry?

What are the *coyotes* charging, human traffickers,
what's the exchange rate
                                on the peso black market?
The skies are cloudless, answerless—
only a distant thunder on the horizon
                                        that tells you it's dove season,
that the white-striped wings will soon be falling.

Those walking the fields will stay invisible—
they will show only as white blazes on X-rays of eighteen wheelers,
lives hidden amidst ripening mangoes,

the unseen body that walks beside you,
like an undertow of feathers,
like a call that disappears
                        the moment it's answered.

Ante Up

tonight at the poker table I counted
a hundred years in the mills
good living   hard life they said

while we waited for the river card
one to burn & one to turn

I could never catch a card to save my life

but somewhere up there's the luck I've heard of
sweet as manna   luck or grace   prayer or
pair of pocket rockets   whatever you want

to call it   that promised land just across
the Jordan   just past the badlands
better lucky than good
better forgotten than lucky   or forgiven
if it's exes or God or the IRS

so I leave my language for leaving
on the table with the one day of rain
this summer   with my words for mercy

& silence &/or God   (who would I speak them to
anyway)   (words that come between me

& God) words as quiet as
whiskey evaporating in barrels   the angels' share

so they say   wherever they are   they walk
with the lives   we might have lived
had the cards fell a little better   I leave it all

on the table   stray bills & lean years & names
of old lovers   & walk out into the night
a possum kingdom of empty streets

Winter Song

In the sound of pellet snow falling
on still-green leaves, magnolia & oak,
I hear ten thousand brushes on the high hat,

someone whispering for Elijah,
                                time scraping ghost towns
from the map.
I hear the last percussive rasp
of the song cut off
                by the bone saw's cry
yesterday in the slaughterhouse.

A vanished song for the vanished,
one for the windows of ice
the wind's cleared from the snow

on the reservoir. Lakeside,
I catch myself thinking the patches
are all the nights we won't get back—
if I look long enough
                        I'll see a face I loved.
I don't know who I'm waiting for.

Childhood friends, old loves.
Maybe my grandfather's face,
unmarked by death.

Maybe the pages of my life's history
in the unreadable scrawl
of the town drunk will appear

in the onyx glass,
color of the night hours
that find my grandmother awake

                              belted to her insomnia.
Give it time. Soon the faces
will begin to surface

like coins, like a well
giving up its wishes. And when they do,

they'll have no more to say
than we do, when I ask them
what this morning is the empty

throat of, what happens to all
flesh, or just what the question is,

                              if our passing's the answer.

Texts Blues

Someone pulls a burning splinter from the devil's thigh
                                        & holds it up to the sun—
August in Texas.
And slides it down the frets to get the dying cicadas going, half wheeze
& half-halted gospel hum,

if it's Blind Willie a hundred years ago, Blind Pilgrim
born a stone's throw from here,
if it's a knife blade sliding down the strings,

Jesus gon' make up my dying bed.
In '45 it was a bed in his burned-out house,
                                       nowhere else to go,
wet bed to keep cool in the Texas summer,
that became his dying bed, when the hospital turned away

a man with malarial fever,
because he was blind, or black, or both.

Preached & sang in the streets
to people he couldn't see,
if my wings should fail me Lord,
                               like the cloud of witnesses
the author of Hebrews says we're surrounded by,
whoever that was,
we might never know.

Here, to this cloud of the wanted & missing who look down
at us from billboards, hushed against

the shimmy-shake of locusts buzzing into the call of the coal train
heading north, armature of the next life,

                                            armature or echo
of the day after our last,
to this cloud add the passengers & crew making an emergency landing
at DFW,
meet me in the middle with another pair.

I was on that flight last week,
can hear the flight attendant saying wear your seatbelt low
like J-Lo wears pants,
                        plane low
over the million white RV hookups at the Texas Motor Speedway
I once thought were headstones,

over the thirty foot monoliths on an unfinished I-35 ramp,
henges of a disappeared people,
highway henges of a road into the sky.

I count up all the times my life's been out of my hands

& arrive at *grace*,
at a number I cannot know,
number of wings that will fail in this world—

how long 'till I'll need you to meet me in the middle
of the air? How long
                        will *faith* mean a belief
in what I cannot see?

Southern Tongues Leave Us Shining

Sister says another day another dollar.
Sister spins in the living room, little feet chirping
on the chipped & faded hardwood,
counted bones & silk of skin in the air then not, shimmer

                                                  & arch,

shimmy & spin, of the air & not. She says teacher says
a crate of tap shoes washed up on a beach somewhere,
someday she'll have a pair. In North Korea, she says,

they have billboards that say We Have Nothing to Envy.
Weightless
shadow on the clapboard walls, only something pressed
of hollow bones could turn like that, living shadow

                                         a thousand socks tied to bal-
loons
are floating across the border right now,
winter socks for the coming cold, for those who have nothing.

Sister, I can hardly hear the voice on the radio from the next room
over your feet, & that's alright,
Little Half-Flame, sometimes driving backwoods gravel I spin the dial

& those voices edge in & out
of me, & I'm glad someone is putting tongue to hunger,
someone who's arisen from a shotgun shack

                                    or one of the fine condos
of Section 8, someone who's traced the tongue marks
in the cans of grease out back, & understands

there ain't much to get us through,
& even if out of earshot, even if the voices travel through us
like the unnumbered particles that Perseid each & every second
                                        through the dark skies
our bodies conceal, I'm glad someone's mumbling the charms
that had a woman's bra wire deflect the bullet last week,
had a blanket save a boy the week before,

a bullet that whistled through wood & drywall
& was stopped at the skin by wool.

Numb-fumbling voodoo, bluebird bones & moonlight,
saint or Santeria, whatever works

in this evening of haloes & absences:
white soap shavings around Martin on his chair
(after whittling all that's not angel from the soap bar),
vigil candles guttering, auraed by the perfect circle
they make of their flames. Sneakers hanging by their laces.
And a cloud of beating mothwings around a streetlight,
                                        little nebula,
heart of dust & wings around blue sodium.

Whatever works, forty ounces or pipe dream,
blue train or jellyroll, whatever the moonlight can make of us,

here where the gandy dancers once flickered by the rails,

sister let these tongues attend us, those we cling to,
o flesh that fails, that falls from another flesh.
Light & dust. Of the air & earth.

Let the rivers run through their throats, fine
alluvium, southern tongues come find us

                                           if the new shoes never show,
if our angels are still out of reach,
earshot & eyeshot,

southern tongues leave us shining
for another day.

III
BYE & BYE I'M GOING TO SEE THE KING

Appalachian Vowels

soften the day's glare a little,
long vowels soft as the footsteps
of the lost regiment said to walk these woods,
soft even through the teeth of a mechanic
with a plug of chaw in his cheek.
He breaks a branch from a dogwood
(in a soil that still gives up musket balls)
next to the empty puddle-shot parking lot,
while we shoot the shit
                                    because the day's done
& the bill's settled. He's as many stitch-lines
on his hands & face as I do—
& in this we are kin, misspent or
well-spent youth. No one knows his time,
or what's around the corner, & in this,
too, we are kin, hundred bones &
twenty-one grams of soul, by one guess.
He scattered his father's ashes
last month upon one of the nameless hills
near here that hold generations—
just a little cloud on the air, he says.
Cloud that opens a hollow in us
where it rains for years,
                                    it's the dead, not
the living, who demand the most.
We bear them as these Blue Ridge mountains
surrounding this hole-in-the-wall garage

bear their dynamited ridges,
                        blue aura
still there though, here to the end
of time, blue shine, some trick of light
& isoprene walking the hills—
lost regiment, blue shades all the way
down to the Nantahala.
I don't know who'll be in the ascension,
but today the dust we are rises,
kicked up off a gravel road by a short box
three fields over,
                        white shroud upon the air
like the shade who came forward from the shades
to greet Aeneas, *have you come at last...*

Auramancy

divination by auras

It's Johnny Cash on the little boombox
I carry as we climb the grain silo ladders to get a bird's eye view
of the town, of our dozen streets,
then the father hen will call his chickens home,

a little eschatology in the early evening—
& you ask, *why divinations* a moment before

you press your hand to your head:
the town blurring on its edges, I know from past episodes,

like static breaking in, like the ghost chatter of phantom birds
on radar, the green flecks no one could explain
moving against the wind.

And the lights, every light begins to drift closer.
Aura, you say, quietly. A migraine coming.

Like reading the red sky at morning, the sailor's warning,
or looking for tomorrow
in chicken entrails, tea leaves, casting locks of hair
                              when the *I Ching* goes missing,
as if your body had a handle on the what's-to-come,
o Cassandra, o Isaiah,

your body somehow tuned to the turning of the days,
the way moths steer by the stars, or animals scatter

                                        to higher ground
before the tsunami hits.
I never answered your question—it was reading the Inferno,
meeting the doomed one by one, being moved

by the damned, yes, because who amongst us hasn't dreamed
a passion that would condemn us to a whirlwind
                                        of bodies,
but it was the fortune-tellers that shook me—
forced to carry their heads in their hands with their gaze fixed
behind them always.
                    And for what.
Trying to look through the signs into
tomorrow. Who hasn't looked to the stars

to see if someone's coming back, who hasn't seen a body
hovering between this world & next
                                in the monarch butterflies
rising from milkweed?
You would have laughed,
but all I wanted was to gather them once,
all those condemned sightseers,
because no father hen was coming to take them home.

Are there other windows into the future
your body can look into? Could you look long enough

to see twelve hundred snow geese falling from the sky over Idaho next week?

We begin to climb down, rung by rung, your eyes
closed, slow as Dante down the devil's back.

Cars shake down Main's cobblestones. A siren blares
in the distance. You might outdo the MRI,
find the invisible tear in a tendon, tease out

the names from the next round of pink slips.
Get us through the day. Steer us, get us

home, so there would be no pile of flowers in the middle
of the street. No boombox on the sidewalk, playing a loop

of the DA reciting charges
against the cops, over & over.

We might know the hands on the litter that will bear us.
We might kiss those hands before we go.

Reliquaries

It's a brand new day, the greasy spoon's sign
has recited each day for the last ten years.

18-wheelers haul their hundred hands of empty space
through an air hallowed by the smoke of a thousand-acre grassfire.

New roads take on the shape of the old
the way rivers tongue the shapes of the drowned, eternal rush hour,
eternal city:

beneath the floodlights on the side of the highway
the blue eye of the welder's torch snaps
open, a circular saw spins, disc galaxy, roulette wheel
if the ball's skipping through the working hours

$\qquad\qquad\qquad\qquad\qquad$ of the rest of their lives,
these workers, then bites into concrete,

$\qquad\qquad\qquad\qquad$ teeth through stone.

Mouth full of cinders,
the earth has begun to reel back
its lines of chlorophyll.
Birch shadows walk on their toes on their way
to nowhere. Bark strips skiff from the sycamores,

$\qquad\qquad\qquad\qquad\qquad$ pale coracles,
& set off into the world. Through a screen of falling
rust-shot leaves it's hard to tell the planes from the planets,

but I know one is flight 90, where last week a man
confided that he's collected over twenty thousand Pillsbury Doughboy dolls.

I tried to remember the name of the horn player
who used to play a club for a plate of spaghetti—something about being in-between
cities, in-between lives & hours,
had left me otherwise wordless, with nothing else to offer,

with nothing more to say about need.

Once, I rounded a corner & came face-to-face
with a naked woman behind a door of glass.
                              I saw her
everywhere I went the next few days,
each time I saw myself in a window. In the canal below.
I read a billboard a mile from the glass door: *Voodoo Inverso:*
someday I will learn the spell
                    to reverse
my trafficker's curse.

Ten thousand days into my life, Lord, & not one more promised.
Ten thousand days & I've nothing

to say in light
of the overpass fire in front of me,

                        as this city drains
from its own windows as the sun rises.

You can take ten thousand steps & get no nearer to heaven,
someone once said, but the smoke

is halfway there. If the overpass is a temple,
it's a Parthenon blueprinted
                        by the stars
that are now fading overhead,
one dedicated to elsewhere,
                        that negative mirror,
a thousand times more air than concrete, more not there
than there: a dozen pillars & a cement roof,

nameless place you only know by the places
you're on the way to: a via negativa

of every place you've been. If the ashes on the air
are inch-long vanishing points of veils,
this temple had a million.

And I'll be its augur. Already I can see the bouquets
& votives left there for its priestess, still buckled

in her Corolla, her name unremembered everywhere.

Silence

Milczenie is the Polish word for silence
that couldn't be translated—
not just silence, but not talking,
keeping quiet—
                    like the other end
of the disconnected rotary phone
in Japan, in a lone phone booth

on top of a hill, outside a cemetery—
or a blue begging bowl held up
to your ear.
As when the mourning doves go still
when I approach. Or how the dog

doesn't move while I wash his each & every paw,
then his belly, the pus
the vet can't explain matted in the winter fur.

Suds in the grass,
& fallen apple petals, the size of beads
on rosaries recovered in the Texas desert,
                         Galilee to Golgotha
in a heartbeat, where
                    are the fingers that counted prayers across
the border, across the years? Always there
& we never see them.
And so every road is an Emmaus road.

I talk so much. How often mercy
seems so far away it's almost
starlight. I've Hikmet on this phone right now

saying we must feel this sorrow
for the world must be loved this much

if you're going to say I *lived* . . .

& again I don't know what to say,

         I'm a word halfway
migrated to another language,

a guitar's shadow,
a hollow bone in red dirt,

I'm footprints left in the Rio Grande.

Nocturne with Fitted Absences

"The book of moonlight is not written yet / nor half begun . . ."
—Charles Wright

Flame-limned shreds of leaf & wood drift on the air
from a wildfire two hollers over
as if the library of Alexandria were burning again,

                                             a shroud of smoke

thrown across the stars. In a moonless backyard
I stoop to pick up clothes fallen from the line,

                                    hands & knees, O Lord,

hands & knees—like the man who paced out the underworld,
if Dante's right, though his name escapes me,

                                  the circles there nowhere near

as perfect as grief's, or joy's—
in this city of cinders,

looking for little patches of dark a little darker than the grass—

only a glint of a letter here, there, as a name, a logo,
somehow picks up light in the lightless yard.

The wind hurries away, talking in its sleep,
stray syllables that must meet somewhere—

& somewhere, in a depth I have known
& cannot know,
sometime this week my unborn child

swallows for the first time, though I cannot remember

if there's even a tongue yet.
I know that somewhere the moon breaches for air.

I know that my bones are the spines of nameless books,

& the pages of our flesh have begun to be recited
in the dark waters,

letters of sugars & proteins through the month-old blood,

tongue, thirst, sleep . . .

Appalachian Farewell

It's sluice & sieve this side of the mountain today,
it's TNT & hill heave, & a long slide,
                                    until this side is the other.
Appalachia's a green speck in the eye
of God, a speck man's been working to remove
for the past century or two,

but for now it's dust in our teeth,
it's a missing mountain shoulder
                                    & a missing vowel in our mouths.

Still, I'd like to see the sluice rise for once,
& the Flesh drift back to Word,
if I had words to describe it—debris settling
on a river's hairpin turn now, the sound of the world falling

back to the world. I'd like to see the coal dust transfigure
into someone whose name is beyond me
                                    (dust still high in the sunlight),
someone too radiant to recognize,
who will speak when I don't know which side I'm on.

The Trick

I've always loved that scene in *The Seventh Seal*
where Jof, poor broke Jof the juggler, rushes back
to tell his wife Mia that he's just seen the Virgin & Child,
so close to me that I could have touched her, but Mia
is skeptical, wants to know what they'll eat this winter,
wants to know how their son Mikael will have a better life.
And Jof says his son will be an acrobat, or a great juggler,
one that can do the one impossible trick—to halt a ball
in midair. Impossible, Mia says. For us, he replies.
But not for him. A trick for the Illusion Hall of Fame,
with the Fabled Bullet Catch, Houdini's vanishing
elephant, or today's, which include the woman who
awoke forty-five minutes after being pronounced dead,
& the lab that created a whirlpool of polaritons,
particles with properties of both light & matter.
Resurrection & transfiguration aside, the trick most days
is just getting through the day. Kids to school on time,
pizza delivered in fifteen minutes, how to leave a bottle
alone. Yesterday my thirty-fourth year left its last glyphs
on the walls of my bones. Today I found out I'm going
to be a father. And today the trick is managing this rising
tide of panic, & excitement, & God knows what else,
as I drive with my wife, five weeks along, to the doctor,
every ache of her past week scrutinized. Each bloodspot.
Impossible one, you'll double in size this week.
And again next week, poppy seed to sweet pea,
if you do not give up. Even the light that enters her eyes
comes to you, as it becomes vitamin D, & reaches you

through the rivers of her body. This is the way light
becomes blood—as the Word, too, became flesh,
we are told. And our words, too, our prayers, must change
flesh—even a body alive in a time before the dream
of language feathers, & unfolds, heart the one still point
in your trembling cloud, yet to start its savage countdown.
Be ceaseless. Turn in that darkness you darken.

IV
SWEETER AS THE YEARS GO BY

Southern Update: Triptych

The FD still doesn't know how the man caught fire.
The PD still doesn't know how an inmate escaped

from the infirmary—a guard had to knock down the door
to the room, only to find translucent tubes thrown

                                        across the empty bed,
blood blown along the needle.
Keep an eye out for him, they say.

But every road's a Damascene road around here,
with this inmate, with the paperless migrants

said to walk the roads & fields beside us (does anyone ever see
them?), & sometimes, when the day's just right

                                        or just gone,
the shades of those driven from their homes in Quakertown
& across the railroad tracks to Salomon's Hill a century ago—

you can guess why—
                        walk through the late evening afterlight
they're stitched of.
Are we all the roads we've crossed in the towns we've lived?
Is that how we'll sum up our lives,
by what we've left behind? Or the sum of our doubts?

We still don't know exactly what brings on labor.
Baby on the way, I don't trust myself
or my doubts, or God, though sometimes

                                    I can't tell them apart.
Tonight I backed away from Him
as if from a bootlegger with a ten gauge.

                              But your soul's the still,
He said, reading my mind,
I'm only the wound I've blown open in you

& the first breath after.
When they emerged from hell
& washed up on the shores of Purgatory, beneath four stars,

                                          light for those
who could not look upon Your light,
Virgil washed Dante's face,

then broke a reed to wear around his waist,
a symbol of humility—you cannot continue

until you realize that you're powerless
to continue. To climb is to surrender each & every moment.

Then another reed grew in its place:
a sanctification attended by a miracle.

Dear Ghost
who walks beside me, in this story I would give everything away,

even prayer,
        if mother & daughter are safe,
I would break for their sakes,
           I pray.
Dear Ghost, the impossible migration
of my wife's organs—her abdominal muscles split in half
& pushed to the side of her ribcage,
               liver & spleen like balloons
against the ceiling of her abdominal cavity—has come to an end.

How do you know when to take her to the hospital,
my father said on the phone to my grandmother
                   when I was on the way.

When she makes you cry to look at her.

And we're there, or almost there, give or take
a minute or two, a contraction, wince, grimace,
               a lone cry
from a room away, dear Ghost, stay close,
              firstborn of the dead
stay close for this birth.
Things become whole once in a while, if you're lucky
or good. Five plates in my daughter's skull are fusing together,
                  right now,
as she descends through the birth canal.

And what does one say to a daughter?

Language is the fire that survives us.

New calves follow their mothers along the fenceline

                                           in the fields outside the city, tail end
of wildflower season,
bean tree blooms bang their drums on the color palette of the world,

magnolia blossoms blaze through waxy leaves, white as the slip

                                            of the devil's wife,
O Lord, their afterimage burning ships

                              that keep sinking out of sight.
This town is every town. Still a long breadline at the foodbank.
Still segregated, by & large,
except for Friday nights, some of us still

                              must raise our young
to raise their hands.

And what does one say to a daughter?

For every pardon, a hundred more in the jug.

For the first glimpse of her head—once
a moon in clouds on the ultrasound,

                            moon that shifts each tide in us—
ten shades in the middle of the street.

For every wet strand of her hair, every word of Ugolino
on his tongue, what it has—no, who
                                        it has tasted.

Letter to My Daughter Perhaps Someday

It's the little things that matter, the gurus & diamond companies
keep telling us. Too often I look through my shoelaces into the earth,

& miss the semaphore of bows & loop-de-loops before I walk out,
today, into a too-early spring day with you, sleeping in one arm.

Secret language of shoes, those little boats you tie up to unmoor,
what conspiracy will it be today, where are they plotting to take us?

Knots, language in which you can untie yourself from the world,
from the likely & the possible, words you can cut in half.

Maybe there's a knot that could stand in for *robin* in Inupiat,
language of the Alaskan Eskimos, since there is no word for robin,

they've never needed one: lariats & trefoils in horsehair or blue ribbons
for nape & tail feather, a Portuguese bowline for hollow bones (is it true

they walk out into the next snowstorm when it's their time to go?).
Last night I dreamed a knot of your hair drifted on a river, just beyond

my reach. A perfect despair. A perfect circle of hair, though that might be
impossible, even electrons have rough edges, even the circles

of the underworld, & the gold record borne on the Voyager spacecraft
that drifts forever, like the Hunter Gracchus, through space,

even that record with one hundred hellos scratched in one hundred
languages has its flaws. Scratched like your face, as you Houdini

out of your swaddle straightjacket & jab yourself with your fingernails
when you startle awake. Love is the dream of the dying, I want to tell you,

or maybe just another dying, some bloodknot of light that weaves us
to each other, but you're beyond language—or yet to recognize it

in your thirty days upon this earth. You wrap your hand around
my finger—a circle, if the diameter is all the days I'll be missing you,

& even in this circle there is an infinite pi that holds our lives somewhere
in its sea of decimals—as it begins to snow on this lonely avenue.

Snows right through my chest when I watch you sleep. What does your
tomorrow look like? What do your dreams look like the day after?

Forgive me my failings. My lack of ambition. I thought my shoes
would take me somewhere. I have no way to tell you what your hair

is like in my hand, on this day, one of the last days I'll have more hair
than you. You may as well be in space, where the earth

is a bluewhite circle far away, a rounded lily, a boutonnière on the lapels
of space. And tomorrow, or a day far hence I hope, a perfect flower

on my dark suit, when I'm laid out, when you let go of my hand.

Nocturne &/or Aubade with Horses

And when a god allowed it to speak
one of Achilles' two immortal horses

                             said a god had killed
its mortal chariot mate, & that Achilles, too,
would be struck down by a god.

And they wept when Patroklos died.
And three midnights now I've waked from a dream of two horses,
brown mare & little sorrel,

                      hardly ten hands high,
that lived next to me when I was a child,

                                    three midnights now
I've waked to walk the windows of the house—
as I once did, as a child, to find my grandmother walking the house,
who learned English by memorizing the Psalms,

                                    I will lay me down in peace & sleep,
for Thou, Lord, only makest me dwell in safety.
Tonight or this morning a mourning dove,
even this late, even this early,

                        poor-mouthing our riches,
our memories, our past days,
even as, there—
& there, my daughter, hardly two hands,
my hands, at two months, cries out in her sleep,

soft as the weeping of a deathless horse.
We dream more in the first three years

of our lives than the rest, but where do they go,
where are the dream horses stabled?
Somewhere close to the mercies we've been shown,
maybe, the ones we didn't deserve.

Tomorrow's already here,
                              on our skin, our tongues,

baker's hour, hangman's,
& I've given up on tonight's,
but there's another sleep, love,
                              one I'm closer to

than you, if all goes right, if we're lucky or good,

& though I've asked the dream horses
when it's my time to go,
they, like Xanthus, like the future itself,
have been struck dumb.

V
LET YOUR LIGHT SHINE ON ME

Southern Divinations II

dog with a dead chicken tied to its neck

copperhead body curled upon a shovel blade
steel gleam between head & body

I want to believe somewhere in the world
her departure was writ before she left

in the geoglyphs wild boars beat through fields
of beans scrub pine & prairie grasses

in the long flares of the magnolia blossoms

blood moon sunk to its throat in the reservoir

the invisible vapor trail the Trinity leaves
as it follows the drought

secret alphabets dove wings scrawl on the air as they fall

though no one ever finishes saying goodbye
I leave the house of mourning with its shrouded mirrors

a little sad the world's first evening without her in ninety-five years
is beautiful   this sudden rain out of nowhere in the midst

of evening sun   wet shine on streets & windshields   deadfall
& little torches of pearl millet

I'll learn the signs one day
read the half-gutted skinned pig hung from a hook in a driveway

doe caught on the fence wires starred with black cow fur

somewhere it's written that my daughter
would find my arms
would find her reflection in the mirror & run her fingers
along her own delighted gaze
                              (trails in the dust smaller than termite bores)
where is it written that one day
she will pull the sheet down upon my days
                              (my span of days between her hand
& her mirror hand) if I was born without a birthright
each body is the beginning of my native land

How Does a Man Become a Hashtag

is it the way air becomes hollow bones inside
doves lifting above a summer field

or the way the flares of mimosa blooms limn the current
of the Frio as it churns beyond the bend

(*white stars fly out from a well-dark barrel*)

is it like alchemy the way your hundred bones transform
into language   is it like pasture flames that sing down
beneath green blades

(*gunpowder residue settles upon your skin*
like pollen dusted on a wing)

is it the way dew rises from long grasses
or like fog above a river
or a little at a time like horse blood drawn
from a tick bite

(*now lie down   now rest*)

the way a loon is part of the lake when it dives into a dark
we've never dreamed
or how the cottonseed meshed within the feeder's wire skeleton

is eaten by deer
& so jumps with the bodies

of these white-tailed ghosts who leap the trails
in front of us   half wind & half-rumor

(red & blue lights strobe across a neighborhood)

are you liminal as the body
who climbs the ladder we've left

                                        at the fence that divides
one country from another

do you become a million points of orange-black light
like the migrating monarch butterflies

do you enter this hieroglyph the way language flowers
in my daughter

all twelve months of her   all hundred-something bones
all the world unsayable but for the sign *enough*

(now the crowd begins to gather)

which is two hands waving at collarbone level
those twin oars scarcely bigger than picks on a comb

if her hands drift any higher
she's signing *applause*
at this world   at this evening   the sudden squall   tiger lilies & purple thistle
full throttle in each ditch & dive in this county

moon's pale shrift upon canyon bones
& exposed white caliche stones

(now lie down   now rest)

rough as sand upon the hands that are saying no

she's signing *enough enough enough*

They Ate the Bulbs of Tulips

I'd have to hear it spoken in mind somehow,
my father said, of the Frisian word for *hunger,*
but I'd settle for *memory,* or *grief,* under
the category of things that undo me. It's a funny
thing to think. Who would be the speaker
if not him? His mother, maybe,
holding hands in the hospital with his father
after seventy-six years. Married the day after the war,
when the stores had no windows—the Nazis
took the glass. The mourning doves
might have the right vowels, or the red belly
in the leafless dogwood, now winging
through the sunlight peplummed through
the pines, blue tarp peeled back
on the cotton bales in the field beyond,
Merry Christmas spraypainted in blue
upon the white. Snowless, starless,
a man goes on trial in France for helping
refugees. Could've been your grandparents,
my father says, your Pake hid in barns, woke
once to mouse feet scrambling across his face,
but in France it was a two-year-old in a ditch,
dying of dehydration, & when I look down
I've pulled the petals from the bouquet,
& as I've neither French nor Frisian nor
courage, all I can do is sweep the body
of petals into my palms, & pour them into
the cathedral of water in front of me.

Prayer for This Day

Through scrub pine & river hickory trees
shafts of sunlight fall
                          sharp as a needle,
if the adrenaline's the open page
on the table,
which says *often and often, father, you would appear to me,*
Your sad shade would appear . . .

no ghosts here, no, & if the Lord of hosts,
no answer to what we ask, bread, or wine,
                                      or why—
though we're listening, asking for a sign, a reply—

even a *not yet*—
& yet, there I was
three stairs down
when my daughter fell,
her body light as a sheaf
                          torn from the Book of Kells.
I don't know that I've done anything better with my life.
I don't know what I'd do without her.

Reach out your hand & put it in my side,
                              my Lord said to the doubter.
And wherever you are, put your hand here:
                                no one was shot in Dallas today.

There's still water in the Trinity
forty days since last rain.

I hold up my student with the immigration hearing to you.
I hold up my daughter's almost-asthmatic lungs.

Tomorrow is easy, Stevens says, today is difficult.
Tomorrow ain't shit, Bubbles echoes,

                                        somewhere on *The Wire,*
no shit, so guide us, Lord,
as we zig the streetside dumpsters & dealers
zag the halfway house,

                        zig the conspiracy theorist
who knows where all the witnesses
to JFK's assassination disappeared to,

zag the stadiums alive in their hundred thousand watt wounds,
our towns desegregated for one night, just one,

                                    so this must be a dream
or an act of God
(how will you bless us?
You said, I will use your poverty—

it's writ plain. Your will be done,
despite all I can't explain).

I hold up this breath. These hands to catch
falling bodies, hands to brush
away the stinging fire ant, open

                        the manual of this EpiPen.

Close your fist around the auto-injector.

Don't close your eyes.

Late Sestet

"a single dog hair can split the wind . . ."
—Charles Wright

We see the shadow of the dog, never the dog itself,
my friend says.

> Meaning the next life, maybe, that beautiful rumor,

meaning God

> or gravity, maybe I'm listening for the whistle, Lord,
that will call me home,
a wind to still the wind
between my ribs,

> where leaves are falling through gray skies . . .

Let It Shine on Me

sings a man who lived his last week
in a burned-out house,
who made his bed in the ashes,

& as he swings from faux-bass guttural of *let your light*
                                        to a slow

clear lifted tenor *shine* with seven seconds left
I ask him how he slept that week,
just last night I spilled sleep meds
on my grandmother's obit.

Why did the hospital close its doors to you,
in 1945, in Beaumont, Texas?
What does forty years of blindness
& dying of malaria
do to a faith that sang *My Lord*
                        He done just what he said—

heal the sick & raise the dead.

The needle skips to *God Don't Never Change*
but I've always believed prayer moves Him,
                                it must.
I've always hoped for a God generous enough
to be wounded by this world,
                        by our segregated churches,

our segregated dead.

Sang & preached in the streets to strangers you couldn't see.
But no healing here. No grave—
lost to the years. At the end, or just after

the end, how did you leave?
Just close your eyes.
Or did the air suddenly smell of rain
& myrrh, as someone led you by the hand

                                 from the roofless
dwelling you made of defiance & cinders
through the streets of sleep

to a house with many rooms,
a vase full of Texas wildflowers,
little lighthouse,
                shining in one?

Southern Tongues Coda (Precision Dying)

"ain't no dark till something shines . . ."
—*Townes Van Zandt*

I don't know what the dog stares at
as I wash the pus from his belly
(pissing blood a week, vet
can't say why), body
                          still enough
to be pointing game,
(is this the soundless way
                          the next life will be bayed?)
or why he chews the early wind-scattered samaras

& long grass beside the drainage ditch
in which three deer in the last three months
                          have come down to die.

Sometimes I feel I'm privy
to just a verse or two from the animal gospels,
though ask just about anyone
working with the near-dead, the almost-gone,

they'll tell you the will
or soul or just plain stubbornness
will keep a person here until they decide to let go.

Precision dying, you might call it.

On her last morning Mama held out
more than four hours,

time enough
to drive Virginia Beach to Raleigh.
I don't know how to make you believe
no hydrangeas bloomed the year she died.

If there are more neurons in the brain than stars
in the Milky Way, where is the Star of Letting Go?

And what does its last light reach as it pulses out.

Some little planet, some field, empty
save a man who washes a dog

in an evening that was promised
to no one, in a twilight that did not invite us.
Soon, the dark river. And a moon like a salt lick half-
tongued down, & still,

        so many iridescent eyes.
This is what we do when we don't know what to do,
when we have little

        but lack or labor in the way of salve.
Wash the body. Say something.

Texts Blues II

And God said, *let there be tinder*
& an August Texas was sparked from flint & stone,
                                        dry as a hog's tongue

two weeks dead, sunstruck thistle & bloomless
blackfoot daisy & fleabane,
chickweed & burweed
                    a deadfall mist
a quarter-inch above every field, empty spillway a snakeskin
curling through town,
                    empty as God's throat.

But this may have been the hour impressionism or baby CPR
was discovered, or the hour our names were written in water

by the lead letters sunk in the Thames a hundred years ago,
or the hour a country was founded—
one that consists of all the No Man's Lands in the world,
                                        every foot

of space between borders.
If I were its creator, I'd start here, with innumerable fields
divvied up with barbed wire, empty
but for oil derricks & longhorns, frack well scaffolding
                                        rising from the scrub,

thin as the ribs of the dead.
Let there be tinder, & there was—
what we did with the hollows between us,
light or heat in a drought-struck heatspell
out of nothing

but a tangle of limbs,

                              which is all I've ever wanted
out of life, or Texas, all I hoped for
until this bobblehead baby showed up,

who flails like a spider monkey
when she's been too long without sleep,

                              baby with a cry that cuts through plaster
& bone, like Chewbacca on a kazoo.
And for song we've a toilet that howls like a kettle

after the flush: maybe we'll never hear the mermaids singing
but listen, the gators of Lake Lewisville are whistling

right up through the pipes of this tumbledown shack,

                              over the echoes
of the train horn, last bell, last call in a few hours.

Let's keep an eye on the life
in our hands, & one on the dream country of the future,

                              that train we've never seen,
on this sickle moon's glint, knuckle
of one of the hands bearing the dark litter westward.

Stray Paragraphs from the Year of the Rooster

Denton, Texas

When the evening light's pale as a butcher
                                    with his mouth sewn closed,

half-moon a bone borne aloft
on a bier of thistle,

the last of the commuters begin to head home on the Texas superhighways—

hell's half acre
                    if we're going by heat,
& if the other half's
our regrets & unkept promises—

home to the suburbs, thinking on the past—
their heads fixed backward,
as if it's the eighth circle
of the underworld,

the one with the fortune-tellers, diviners,
the ones who couldn't see it coming.

Did they see a woman returning yesterday
                                    to the slave cabin she was born in,
eighty-seven years in between these two days?
Or Charlie Murphy tweeting *release the past to rest*

as deeply as possible
                    the night before he died?
One to sleep on, it began. Another one
to sleep on—

the ashes of Bob Probert sprinkled in the penalty box
at the Joe, before they tore it down.
He fought with a grinning heart
                    & a right hand like a hammer, never mind

the feather, the heart will be weighed against
what we turned away from,
                    who we couldn't face.

There's a black cat fix for every frack well,
someone said
before we voted on drilling this town,
                    but there's none for remorse,
only long grass on the grave of the shooters,
the famous ones,
                    the ones who hit the Indians from a mile out,
long grass & a high noon,
so it's about the time
Christ forgave the penitent thief—

so maybe there is a fix.
Or maybe eternity's a rain-wrapped angel come down
to tell you there's no eternity. Sometimes
                              he's selling oranges
on the freeway onramp for a dollar.
A buck, then the otherworldly scent, citrus
or myrrh. After hunger, & the world, & the self itself,

the last renunciation is the smallest,
smaller than a snakebite.

And the door to heaven is even smaller,
if you can find it,
                    locked except to the touch,
& if you do, remember me.

And the moon, from Jordan
to Jerusalem, clear as chrism oil
                         half a second after the blessing,
the moon sets even in hell,
even here, one to sleep on,

with nothing but new blooms
for company, new blooms &

a little rain out of nowhere, just now,
empty streets & the company of heaven.

Letteromancy (The New Causality)

divination by cast letters

And the mile the wildfire ember travels on the wind.

And the mile of blood tides through the capillaries & arteries
                                                    of my daughter's body,
& the empty towns that wait for faces in each
of the chambers of her heart.

And the mile in that last inch between the end of me
                                        & the hem of His garment, good Lord,
may as well be a thousand here on Mile 627,
hwy 20—a little east of Carthage in west Louisiana—
a black stripe through fifty acres of head high afterfire shrub

punctuated by a handful of bonepale trees,
three- & four-story antler-bare survivors.

My daughter's asleep in the childseat, as the headlights winnow
the road from the dark, like the twin beams of light

in the Double Slit Experiment, which showed that future measurements
somehow affected the state of the photons in the past,

as they were setting out. So when I lean back & twist to press
the back of my hand to her forehead

& see the shadow letters UNIVERSITY cast by the rear window sticker
against the moonlight,

it's her degree I'm seeing some twenty years later, her marriage
& the faces of her kids luminous between the letters.

What future events & coming lives have left their prints on this instant,
this one instant? I've turned for just a moment

                                           & yet by the time I turn back
from the rest of her life

                        this present moment runs like water through my hands.

A man has walked out of Angola prison after forty years.
Ornette Coleman dies. Twenty thousand stars drift out of the reach
of our telescopes, if the math on the expanding universe holds,

this stripe of road blazes west

& the fever in her body sets fire to Carthage two thousand years ago.

Aubade with Horses (Fort Worth Impromptu II)

There's no right word for the color of the ashes,

you said, at the New Orleans hospice—
every week a new urn carried out
& poured into the nameless garden.

Maybe it's true. And maybe,
just there through the fog,
this morning's mare & her foal,
                              gray-dappled & steaming,
comes close enough.
Or the grime-dulled silver of the quarter you were given once
to dig a horse grave—
a piano's worth of handthrown earth,
when you were young, first of many.

A quail flailing skyward might come close,
or the color of an unanswered prayer, or the first mouthful of gob,
sucked & spat out from the rattlesnake bite
before the blood hits.

And if the horses are the ashes, this sundog's
                              the transfiguration,
southeast of the sun, toward Nacogdoches,
dragonfly glimmer that Sherwin-Williams might call
skin-at-the-soprano's throat, if she's under the bright lights,

if her last aria is on our forgetting,
& how the language fails us, as it so often does.

O cloud of flesh, o dream
of rain out of cloudless skies,

                              we begin to be erased
when we lose the graves,
when we lose the tongues.

Someday we'll know how to mend the horse's bones
without driving her mad.

Someday we'll come to the green pastures,
where we'll be poured out, & the lost vowels

                              will fall back to our tongues like snow.

Biographical Note

Mark Wagenaar is the author of *The Body Distances (A Hundred Black-birds Rising)* (University of Massachusetts Press, 2016). He is the 2014 winner of the Pinch Poetry Award, the New Letters Poetry Prize, and the Mary C. Mohr Poetry Prize, as well as the 2013 winner of the James Wright Poetry Prize, the Poetry International Prize, and the Yellowwood Poetry Prize. Wagenaar's poems have been published or accepted by *32 Poems, Field, Image, The Missouri Review, Ninth Letter, Shenandoah, Subtropics,* and *Washington Square*. He teaches at Valparaiso University and lives in Valparaiso, Indiana.